COUNSELLING IN RELIGION AND PSYCHIATRY

UNIVERSITY OF
NEWCASTLE UPON TYNE
PUBLICATIONS

COUNSELLING IN RELIGION AND PSYCHIATRY

The Riddell Memorial Lectures
Forty-third Series
delivered at the
University of Newcastle upon Tyne
on 10, 11, and 12 November 1971

BY

DESMOND POND
Professor of Psychiatry
The London Hospital Medical College
University of London

LONDON
OXFORD UNIVERSITY PRESS
1973

Oxford University Press, Ely House, London W.1

GLASGOW NEW YORK TORONTO MELBOURNE WELLINGTON
CAPE TOWN IBADAN NAIROBI DAR ES SALAAM LUSAKA ADDIS ABABA
DELHI BOMBAY CALCUTTA MADRAS KARACHI LAHORE DACCA
KUALA LUMPUR SINGAPORE HONG KONG TOKYO

ISBN 19 713912 4

Printed in Great Britain
at the University Press, Oxford
by Vivian Ridler
Printer to the University

TO HELEN

PREFACE

I AM deeply grateful to the University of Newcastle upon Tyne, and the Riddell Memorial Lectures Committee for the honour conferred upon me by their invitation to deliver the Riddell Memorial Lectures contained in this book. As will be seen, my interpretation of the intention of these lectures is more practical and less scholarly than those of my distinguished predecessors. An interdisciplinary study has of necessity to be superficial within the space of three lectures, but I hope that the unifying theme of one patient's predicament standing for that of us all, will give these lectures coherence and relevance.

D. A. P.

London,
March, 1972

CONTENTS

LECTURE I

LECTURERS under the Riddell Memorial Trust are required to deal with a contemporary subject in relation to natural theology. Many psychiatrists have written about religion with little agreement amongst themselves as to its function and meaning in the lives of people. My first thoughts gave rise to the title 'The Deserted Temple' which suggests some late eighteenth-century gothic novel or romantic painting—a tale of outdated passion set amidst medieval arches or broken classical columns. To a certain extent my lectures are about past emotions and outdated myths, but they are more an inquiry into why the Temple has become deserted and what might be happening to those human emotions and actions that used to find their fulfilment in a way of life centred on a religious culture. This first lecture will discuss how the traditional professions of law and medicine formulate people's psychological problems and their ways of dealing with them. These professions are often ineffective because I believe that they are usually deficient in their approaches to basic human nature, both as regards their psychological understanding of the individual and their own roles in society.

The second lecture will deal with the newer professions of social work and psychology, especially in regard to education and their possible roles in the prevention of psychological disturbance, as well as their management, once such upsets occur. I shall here describe the rise of the concept of counselling and the changing roles of the personal service professions in our society. The Kilbrandon and Seebohm Committee Reports[1] and their subsequent implementation are both the product of and stimulus to changes in the ways of helping people with their ordinary, but frustrating and debilitating human problems.

The third lecture will deal more specifically with the philosophies underlying these different approaches, and how changes in these deeper ways have led to the Temple becoming deserted.

Behind the organizational differences of the professions are important changes in our understanding of man's nature and its development, both biologically and socially (in so far as these can be separated). Recent Western society has hovered between the euphoria of Rousseau's noble savage and the damnation of Original Sin. We can now deal more knowledgeably with our own upbringing, and I hope to show that these new approaches must profoundly affect some of our social structures, especially the older professions of the law, education, medicine and, above all, the Church.

In a more theological age Corpus Christi might aptly summarize all I have to say—the Body of flesh and blood; the Body of social organization, and the mystical Body of the sacrament, and how they have interacted in the past. My main theme is why we have to find new ways of their interaction, yet preserving the psychological continuity of body, society, and

[1] *Local Authority and Allied Personal Services Report*, Comnd 3703 (London, H.M.S.O., 1968). These Reports formed the basis of the legislation (Local Authority Social Services Act 1970) setting up the new enlarged social services departments.

sacrament. But the Body of flesh and blood; nature, and even man, has no longer to be propitiated as it is already controlled or, at any rate, controllable. As regards society—the Body of social organization—we have to operate more knowledgeably and in less hierarchical and institutional frameworks. For as much as the sacrament expressing the mystical Body, we may soon be living in a world where human traditions and history are no longer moulding us with a solid artistic inheritance of stone, word, and sound, that provides the material basis of any symbolism.

I am beginning with the medical equivalent of a parable—a case history, an actual human problem from which to draw some general conclusions and also test more theoretical approaches. The young man's story I shall quote is one in which the law, medicine, and education have ineffectively tried to intervene.

William, aged 14, was the son of a professional man, sent to me because of persistent bad temper, disobedience, and recently clandestine pot-smoking, resulting in removal from his public school. He was a big, physically mature boy who, three years previously, had had a single typical major epileptic seizure for which no obvious cause had been found. He had been treated with anticonvulsant drugs during the following year, with no clear effect for better or worse on his long-standing awkward personality. While in my waiting-room, he had a tremendous scene with his parents, shouting that it was society that was sick and not he who was being made to see the psychiatrist. Shortly after my first interview, he was arrested in another city for being in possession of cannabis. The magistrate, anxious to maintain provincial respectability, was keen to make an example of one of these London drop-outs, but was able to be persuaded to put the boy on probation as long as he was attending a special boarding-school for intelligent delinquent boys. At first the parents seemed good, tolerant, understanding people, but marital tensions became more apparent as the boy started to get better, and problems involving the whole family began to unfold in ways I shall describe in more detail later.

This short case history shows in miniature the practical problems which give rise to the theoretical topics that I want to discuss. What was wrong with William? Was he ill, in the medical sense, with a disease of the brain that might also have produced a fit a few years before? Was he just a no-good layabout, spoiled by indulgent parents, as the magistrate saw him? Was he just an ordinary adolescent, unsure of his role in society, desperately trying to establish his own identity *vis-à-vis* his parents? Was he right after all, and it is we who are sick and he the sane and sensible one in refusing to conform to our decadent social structure?

All the great traditional professions, medicine, law, religion, and education have been involved in trying to make people better physically and/or morally. For the most part they used methods voluntarily agreed to by society, though not necessarily acceptable to the client at the time of suffering them. I shall largely leave out mass methods, such as politics and similar social activities aimed at us all, and not only when we feel in need of help, although many techniques in these fields are common to those that will be discussed. The influence of the mass media on the traditional ways of the professions will, however, have to be mentioned later.

Some may straight away take issue with this idea that the professions are concerned with making people better. Is not the law fundamentally concerned with justice and only in a minor area—penology—involved in making people better? Is not education concerned with the inculcation of knowledge and the capacity to think, and only in part with character building? Are not all religions, including Christianity, involved in understanding and trying to control the world, and in carrying a Gospel to those whose conversion to the Truth may not make them better as the world sees it? Nevertheless, I believe that it is right that, more and more, people are concerned with the good or ill effects of these professions.

These lectures are also a study about Ends and Means in the sense that Aldous Huxley used these words in his classic book. Perhaps, better still, they are about Beginnings, Ends, and Means, since I hope to consider the particular difficulties of prevention rather than treatment, deterrence rather than reform, early education rather than later re-education, and the natural growth of a religious view of life rather than sudden conversion.

Furthermore, it is useful and meaningful to discuss these vast and apparently different areas of social activity because I believe that in addition to common Ends they have certain common psychological and social Means behind their great differences of language and technique and in their manifest roles in society. I am particularly concerned with areas in which more than one profession is involved; for example, in the treatment of offenders with which medicine and penology are concerned; in child guidance in which medicine and education must both interact.

I am, of course, greatly influenced by Professor Paul Halmos[1] for his delineation of the personal service professions in which he includes clergy, doctors, nurses, teachers, social workers. These he contrasts with the impersonal service professions of lawyers, accountants, engineers, architects. You will note that Halmos puts the lawyers among the impersonal service professions, whereas I include the law in the professions which we have to consider because of its concern with the reform and deterrence of criminals.

I want to start with describing some aspects of the practice of medicine, being most familiar with my own profession. Most civilizations, or, at any rate, the more advanced ones, have had more or less independent professions of medicine, made up of men who were skilled in certain practical arts, such as surgery, and knowledgeable in the effects of drugs. Though physicians and surgeons were only comparatively recently formally unified in the Medical Acts of 1850, they were always recognizably different from the other professions in that both dealt with disorders of the body. However, their practice has always included a dimension which differentiated their activity from veterinary medicine; namely, they take account of patients' symptoms—their subjective complaints—as well as the objective signs of bodily disorders; and their interests extend into the 'mental' to a varying and ill-defined degree.

[1] Paul Halmos, *The Faith of the Counsellors* (Constable, London, 1965); Paul Halmos, *The Personal Service Society* (Constable, London, 1970).

One of the main effects on medicine of the nineteenth-century scientific revolutions was an apparent rigidification of the concept of a Disease. Patients suffered from hard and fast clinical entities, the most clear-cut being those that are caused by infective agencies like typhoid fever. Malformations and mal-developments, physical damage (trauma), degeneration, and new growths (cancers) are the other main pathological groups. All these concepts appeared at first to fit most physical disorders satisfactorily. But this view is changing, especially as our knowledge grows of the ways whereby the patient responds biochemically and physiologically to noxious organisms or agents, like bacteria or poisons. Medicine is now moving to a more biological concept of disease as a process, meaning such things as the effect of interaction between the chemistry or metabolism of host and parasite in infection, or the effect of changing metabolism within an organism during prenatal development or senescence.

Confidently armed with all this knowledge, medicine invaded the spheres of mental disorder, but with conspicuously less satisfactory results. Infections, malformations, degenerations, and new growths appear to account for only a small proportion of mental disturbances. Physicians were also forced to look again at patients as distinct from their diseases. Not only was mental illness not understood, but the improvements and relapses of many chronic physical disorders were incomprehensible without seeing the human organism as one capable of learning patterns of behaviour. Even the most mechanistic doctor recognizes, at an elementary level, that mental states can produce bodily changes, even if only when he panics at an examination and can feel his heart racing, his hands sweating, and he has an urgent desire to pass water. The ramifications of psychological influences on bodily changes, especially the more chronic ones that may lead to irreversible physical damage, have been systematically analysed only comparatively recently.

There are also, of course, effects in the opposite direction. Many bodily processes influence our thoughts and feelings; in particular, the universal phenomena of maturation and then degeneration of the body (and especially the brain) subtly influence our psychological development and then deterioration from birth to death. The fact that mind and body are indissoluble is the reason why physicians must always be concerned in some way with many aspects of the behaviour of their patients.

The corollary, however, is that medical practice and theory are therefore influenced by the laws of psychological activity. Complaints, even signs as well as symptoms, cannot be understood without seeing them in a social setting. Even more revolutionary is the idea that the doctor's behaviour *vis-à-vis* his treatment of illness, is also not understandable solely in terms of his applying objective skills, such as prescribing a specific drug, or performing a particular operation. His actions have a psychological effect on the patient and conversely the patient's attitudes can influence him.

For a long time psychiatrists have been fighting for the concept of mental illness as describing conditions analogous to medical illnesses which cause aberrations of behaviour. The disease concept has been useful in some respects; for example, in fostering research into drugs which influence the mind. The triumphs of psychopharmacology in the treatment of depression, for example, are undeniable, but general acceptance of this concept in psychiatry has been a Pyrrhic victory.

In the first place, the disease concept in medicine is undergoing a metamorphosis. Physical illnesses are now analysed in terms of the physiological and biochemical disorders of organs and systems of the body. The patient no longer has *a* Disease with *a* Cure, but, for example, the mechanisms of breathlessness are analysed, and to a certain extent some of them can be corrected; what was called 'toxaemia' or 'general malaise' is broken down into various alterable biochemical changes; the reason why the host's resistance to the invading organism has broken down can be investigated and sometimes improved. It follows from this that in the case of mental illness we have to go back to further analysis and understanding before real advances can be expected, and it is an open question whether the methods of investigation appropriate to most physical illness apply to most psychiatric disturbances. To label a person ill rather than possessed or criminal does no more than make it easier for society to see him as a subject for research and understanding rather than as someone to be summarily dealt with.

Secondly, the great complexity of modern medicine has meant that the medical man is now only one person involved in the patient's care. Up to a dozen people may be simultaneously involved in caring for a patient during major surgery—nurses, anaesthetists, electronic engineers, biochemical technicians—many of them doing skilled work not learned without a science degree and postgraduate study. The patient is processed by team-work, co-ordinated usually by the medical man. The team-work for the management of mental disorder spreads far into the social and educational fields, and it is questionable who should be in charge.

Thirdly, the disease concept has encouraged the idea in some people that mental illness is a condition which doctors can treat and cure without any effort on their own part, other than faithful collaboration with whatever treatment regime the doctor prescribes.

At the present time one can discern two trends influencing the place of medicine in society but in opposite directions. On the one hand, the prodigious achievements in medicine in virtually eliminating many physical illnesses, like smallpox, and the power of controlling most others has raised the status of the medical profession so that it appears to be almost omniscient and omnipotent. Yet, on the other hand, and perhaps not altogether paradoxically, as the mysteries of disease are cleared up, the physician's prestige as a magician is less now than when his therapeutic armamentarium had much less power. Medicine has shared in the diminishing of traditional authority figures that is occurring at the present time almost universally. Much of the irritation and dissatisfaction felt by general practitioners, especially, in the National Health Service, is due not just to the conditions of service as such, but to the changing role that doctors have in our society. Similar parallel changes in attitudes are occurring, for example, in America, with a totally different medical system. A beneficent effect of the loss of the mystiques of medicine has been that we are now able to see more clearly what social and psychological roles doctors have played in the past which may not have any necessary connection with bodily disease.

To be ill means also to enact a social role.[1] The rules as regards, for example, behaviour in hospital, are fairly well known and, by and large, adhered to by amateurs and players alike. But the roles as played in medical and surgical wards do not apply appropriately to psychiatric wards. In the latter there is no stereotyped bedside manner, no unalterable patient dependency on doctor who is thought to know best, but to a greater or lesser extent, according to the knowledge and skill of the psychiatrist, the patient's role while in the psychiatrist's care is seen as mirroring his behaviour in everyday life. The doctor/patient contact is constantly used as a learning situation. There are times that may require the therapist and the patient to enact some very primitive and childish relationships indeed, as will be discussed further in the later lectures.

The important point is that the psychotherapeutic situation is at one end of a regular continuum. The other end is represented by the impersonal surgical operation on the anaesthetized patient. Doctors and patients move up and down that line according to their personal skills and the requirements of the medical condition. The continuum between medicine in the narrow sense and psychological treatment, is not the only one. There are parallel continua, for example, in

[1] The sociology of medicine has a rapidly expanding literature mainly from the United States and stemming largely from Talcott Parsons. Those interested will find *Medical Sociology* by David Mechanic (Collier-Macmillan, New York, 1968) a good introduction.

law or education, that might throw light on the individual and social processes involved in psychological treatment which I shall describe later.

To illustrate these points let us return to our patient, William, for whom the narrow medical approach had proved useless, if not actually misleading and harmful. The first formulation of his disorder as due to disease of the brain, and the drug treatment that resulted from it, was of no help. Nor would it have been of help to ascribe the disturbance to just puberty, since this is something we all pass through without necessarily breaking down. In the second phase of the approach to his troubles their psychological nature was recognized only as an intra-psychic disorder; i.e. William was treated in isolation from his family in an excellent school for maladjusted children. He, himself, is improving, but relapses regularly on returning home, while his parents still flounder without any very clear help being given to them in understanding their role. This causes difficulties, not only for William, but for the psychological development of his younger brother and sister who are already showing signs of stress.

To look beyond the individual patient to the factors in society that have led to his becoming diseased has proved surprisingly difficult for doctors trained in traditional medical schools. Even in the heyday of the disease concept in medicine, public health had quite a struggle to gain acceptance in the medical profession. Only in comparatively recent years have the powerful research techniques of epidemiology been widely applied, with important results in our understanding and sometimes control of many diseases besides the epidemics of infections that began this type of research. The application to mental disorders has been less fruitful, except at a comparatively elementary level of symptom-counting.[1] The main reason for this failure is that few psychological disorders can be understood as due to infections or as transmissible genetic disturbances, or resulting from noxious environmental stimuli. The treatment and prevention of much mental disorder does not follow the same patterns as does the care of medical conditions. Psycho-prophylaxis has finally burst the seams of traditional medicine, and to try and understand it we have to turn to psychological and sociological concepts that owe nothing to medicine in the narrow sense, as I will describe in my second lecture.

It may seem rather quixotic to assert that psychological healing will gradually become divorced from medicine at the very time when the taking of drugs of one sort or another seems to be virtually universal, but I believe this should be a most important step to greater psychological maturity in us all. (Perhaps we need a new teetotalism—a signing of the pledge to eschew not just alcohol but all psycho-active drugs.)

How would William's problem have been seen if he had been presented to the courts simply as a straightforward juvenile delinquent without the background knowledge of his medical and family history? This leads us to

[1] It is instructive to compare the different approaches to the nature and prevalence of mental disorder of psychiatric epidemiologists like M. Shepherd *et al.* in *Psychiatric Illness in General Practice* (O.U.P., London, 1966) with the non-statistical, dynamic approach to general practitioners' interactions with their patients in *The Doctor, his Patient and the Illness*, by Michael Balint (Pitman, London, 2nd edn., 1964).

a general consideration of how the law sees the human mind. I am here considering not transactional matters, such as the conveyancing of property, regulation of finance, and so on, but personal misbehaviour—the ways in which society deals with people who have transgressed the law in one way or another, whether criminally or not. It is in this latter sense that I think, contrary to Halmos, that the law is a personal and not an impersonal service profession. The sharpest contrast, even a conflict, with medicine, occurs over the matter of responsibility. The law assumes, until proved otherwise, that the transgressor has, as it is said, 'mens rea'; it is assumed that he knows the law, that he knows he is doing wrong, and that he is fit to take whatever sentence the law in its wisdom passes. Until comparatively recently, the arguments between doctors and lawyers as regards responsibility for major crime were bedevilled by the straightjacket of the McNaghten Rules. Even though these have been largely by-passed, and in spite of Lady Wootton's[1] well-aimed criticism at the whole notion, eminent lawyers, such as Hart, continue to occupy themselves with trying to define the concept of responsibility.

Twenty years ago one of my distinguished predecessors as Riddell Lecturer, Sir Walter Moberly,[2] outlined some of the changes in society's attitude to the law, or rather to the criminal, that he regarded as necessary and inevitable. He pointed out that in the

[1] Barbara Wootton, *Social Science and Social Pathology* (George Allen & Unwin, London, 1959).

[2] Walter Moberly, *Responsibility*. The Riddell Lectures for 1949 (O.U.P., London, 1951). He has recently treated the whole subject in greater depth in *The Ethics of Punishment* (Faber, London, 1968).

Middle Ages canon law was more varied and flexible than civil law, and church discipline milder than its secular counterpart. But perhaps, more clearly twenty years ago when he wrote than now, the established Christian view of guilt, sin, and responsibility, seemed harsher and more rigid than the newer secular psychological approach. Retribution, especially divine retribution, is of diminishing importance in our thinking about the role of punishment; of more importance are reformation of the criminal and the deterrence of others. Moberly considered that responsibility in the legal sense is based on a compound of expediency and morality, and is in itself the raw ingredient of a justice that is designedly crude. He quotes the eminent lawyer, Kenny, as saying, 'The law courts must content themselves with just so much of the truth as is sufficiently obvious to the populace, and make its assertion by physical force not only right but also politic; but the administration of the law is deliberately impersonal—it is not based on the searching moral judgement, the individual criminal or on the supposed mentality of the average man.' One can sense general feeling growing against such crude ideas, nor do many people any longer subscribe to the view held by eminent Victorians, such as FitzJames Stephen and Carlyle, that there is a moral right to hate criminals. Perhaps only in wartime does one now hear such sentiments expressed without guilt in Western society towards large groups of people. However, the fact that capital punishment carries the approval of a majority of ordinary people (to judge by opinion polls) it is clear that there is more change in the judiciary who administer the law, and in the

Home Office who carry out the sentence imposed, than in the public at large as regards attitudes to the individual who commits capital offences. Denis Chapman's book, *Sociology and the Stereotype of the Criminal*,[1] is somewhat polemical, but nevertheless convincingly shows the sense in which society gets the criminals it deserves. We see here a process analogous to the definition of a disease in medicine in the sense that both the disease role and the criminal role are social stereotypes.

Criminal responsibility is a particular example of the general sense in which responsibility is conferred or imposed upon us as a result of the role we play in society. To use Hart's example, we say, rightly, that a ship's captain is responsible for his ship and we expect him to act in a certain way, at times quite heroically, in this role. Once a man is chosen to play a role, the question of his personal or mental fitness to carry it out is raised only in extreme cases of incompetence. Responsibility in the ordinary sense is defined rather negatively by Hart[2] as 'answerability, in the sense of answering or rebutting charges or accusations which, if established, can carry liability to punishment, blame or other adverse treatment'. This relates responsibility to a questionable society activity—the individual efficacy of punishment as a means of modifying behaviour in our

[1] Denis Chapman, *Sociology and the Stereotype of the Criminal* (Tavistock Press, London, 1968).

[2] H. L. A. Hart, *Punishment and Responsibility* (Clarendon Press, Oxford, 1968). The quotation is on p. 265 in the notes on chapter IX. My brief comment does less than justice to Hart's subtle and wide-ranging discussion, though many of the difficulties he faces could probably be resolved more simply and effectively if the law took a less punitive view of responsibility.

society. Punishment certainly does work as a deterrent in a great many areas of social behaviour, perhaps many more than utopian theorists would care to believe, but it has not proved to be of much use in reforming major deviants. Simple punishments for minor offences—for example fines for minor motoring offences—are effective for the vast majority of people, because such people wish, on the whole, to conform to society's rules, and value the sense of belonging to the larger community, with the benefits that this confers. However, if the criminal and/or mentally ill have no such desire to conform and/or no will to reform, then punishment in this sense will not only be ineffective but at times positively harmful in still further alienating the offender from society. In other words, we cannot be content just with the social role concept of crime as social deviance, if we are to understand the criminal mind and prescribe the most effective means of reform and deterrence. We have to relate the roles to their part in the particular criminal's mind.

Seaborn Jones[1] points out that it is more constructive to think of responsibility, not as answerability to punishment in Hart's sense, but as responsiveness in the experimental psychological sense; that is to say, a responsible person is one who has a strong ego in relationship to his own less organized impulses (the id) and to his superego as representative of family and some aspects of society; i.e. responsibility has to be defined in relation both to internal factors of personality structure and to external aspects of his role in society. The responsible

[1] G. Seaborn Jones, *Treatment or Torture* (Tavistock Press, London, 1968).

person is one who can form strong positive attachments to people, groups and/or ideas for which he will make sacrifices and to which, therefore, he is amenable to praise or blame. This can be explicitly compared with the way in which a child relinquishes an immediate and instinctive gratification from fear of loss of love from the parent—a point which I shall elaborate later. Punishment by society is effective only if the individual values society's goodwill; impersonal punishment by strangers, as in prison, is of little psychological value. It is as useless as expecting cathartic relief from telling one's psychiatric history to a tape-recorder.

Just as changes in the Mental Health Act allowing voluntary treatment opened up the possibility of treating mental disorder as a social rather than a purely medical phenomenon, so changes in legislation affecting suicide, murder, divorce, abortion (and probably soon, euthanasia) have opened up more clearly the ways in which antisocial behaviour can be seen to be produced not by any innate criminality or individual original sin, but by various social and psychological forces.

The impact of what Moberly called the psychological view of delinquency has, of course, been much greater in dealings with juveniles than adults. What to do with the concept of responsibility in childhood has always bothered the law. The age at which children could be hanged for crimes has been progressively raised, but the changing attitude to juvenile crime has led to some uncomfortable confrontations, in my view, largely because both medicine and the law have had entirely inadequate concepts of personality.

One of the difficulties arises from confusions of meanings of the word 'guilty'. Victor White,[1] some years ago, clearly spelled this matter out. Lawyers like Hart, and for that matter, Seaborn Jones, too, used the word 'responsibility' explicitly with reference to actions such as committing a criminal act. In this sense, a man may be guilty of crime, but the word 'guilt' goes further than just implying that there is some objective condition such as transgressing the law of the country, infringing the moral code, or committing a sin against God. The word 'guilty' usually implies also that subjective psychological experience of a sense of having committed wrong. Yet those familiar with criminals know well that many of them have no such subjective sense of guilt at all; in fact, they are often just angry against society whom they entirely blame. On the other side, in many patients with mental disorder, especially if depressed, there may be a profound sense of guilt of having committed numberless, if vague, crimes. At times, such a sense of irrational guilt may seem quite abnormal to others, though it may lead the sufferer to do penitential good works that can be valuable socially. By our standards, the lives of the more ascetic saints have been filled by a quite morbid sense of guilt, yet the power for good that some of them have had, at least over their contemporaries, cannot be denied.

In any one person, the development of which particular acts or thoughts are associated with feelings of guilt or, alternatively, of pleasure and satisfaction, can be understood only by minute psychological analysis

[1] Victor White, *God and the Unconscious* (Collins, London, 1960). See also the chapter, 'Guilt: Theological and Psychological' in *Christian Essays in Psychiatry*, ed. Philip Mairet (S.C.M. Press, London, 1956).

of that particular person's life history back to the earliest months of childhood. On the other hand, we also know that crime is not only related to psychological maladjustment in the past. Such an analysis is a prerequisite for the prescribing of the deeper psychological methods of changing behaviour, whether the context of this is medical, penological, educational, or psychotherapeutic—a point to which I will return later. There are criminal gangs, and the socio-psychological analysis of their origins and social cohesion must be undertaken if they are to be overcome. The familiar pattern of social reform for many years can be seen as bringing the Outsider back into society, whether the Outsider has been in the past regarded as criminal or lunatic. Yet, as symbolized by Albert Camus's novel, if nothing else, the Outsider has a social role. Amongst other things, most societies still need somebody outside on whom to project much badness in order to achieve psychological stability for themselves. Whether this projective tendency can ever be overcome is another matter. The current tragedy is that for many people, even whole societies, the Outsider has a different coloured skin—surely the most irrational division of all.

In conclusion to my first lecture, therefore, I should like to come back to William again. In what ways, if any, has our discussion of the legal concept of responsibility helped us to elucidate his troubles? The disturbances of adolescence, that borderland between childish dependence, and adult responsibility, highlight what I have to say about social roles. Adolescents desperately need a social identity; they cling together in gangs whose ethos is dramatically and self-consciously different from the rest of society's, in order to prove that they can be separate people. If the ethos of these groups seems antisocial, as was the possibility in William's case with his drug-taking, then we speak of criminal gangs. If their ethos is high-minded and apparently devoted to good works by identification with the underprivileged or other groups, then their extravagant and unreal character is often not only condoned by society but positively encouraged. The psychological structure of both types of these groups and the long-term effects may, however, bear certain resemblances to each other and, therefore, the moral judgement on the different values of the two groups not correspond to psychological reality.

It is being increasingly widely recognized that the laws concerned with fixing guilt and responsibility on one particular person can result in serious distortions of justice. There are certainly special and peculiar difficulties in the concept of group responsibility. Some philosophers, for example H. D. Lewis, insist that there is no such thing, since responsibility arises from moral decisions, and these can be taken only in the privacy of the individual soul. Society, however, can function only if members of groups can be held responsible collectively for their special duties. The older professions or groups like the army, have solved their problems as they go along with training schedules, ethical codes, standing orders, etc., whose degrees of rigidity are clearly closely related to the general structure of the group. In looser groups, the appropriate sanctions for disobeying the rules may at times seem incomprehensible to the unfortunate members of the groups who suffer some form of punishment. For example, during the transition from family to school, the child becomes aware of class responsibility in a certain sense when teacher keeps them all in as a punishment for the misbehaviour of a few of their members. In other areas of life some penalties may seem equally crude; for example, fining company directors for infringing the Finance Acts, or, as occurred a few years ago, a judge's threat to jail the town clerk of a recalcitrant city council that persistently disobeyed a court order to stop polluting rivers. This last case is a rather bizarre example of the way in which one member of a group often plays the role of scapegoat—a function which has been more or less understood as indispensable in most societies, however unpleasant it happens to be for the particular individual playing the role at the time.

The dangers of such a concept are, of course, that individual members of such a group may deny their individual responsibility for antisocial, immoral, or criminal acts committed by the group. Jean Paul Sartre, in particular, deals with this point, speaking of 'mauvaise foi', or bad faith, when people pretend that some action committed as a senior member of a group, is necessary when it is in fact voluntary. It was generally felt that the international trials of the war criminals in the 1940s were of only doubtful value. My concern here, however, is not with problems such as these on the grand scale of nations; rather I am concerned with showing up the difficulties that the law has in coming to terms with group responsibilities for personal misdemeanours. Society recognizes family responsibilities in many positive ways; for example, family allowances, and many legal rights and duties of parents for their children. However, if a child transgresses the law, attempts to involve the parents in the child's 'punishment' by fining them are of dubious value.

The psychiatrist's special insights into group behaviour come from his knowledge of therapeutic groups in hospitals and the community. In them one can see the same separation of subjective feelings of guiltiness and objective responsibility for actions that I have already described in individual persons. Understanding these interactions takes us far away from medicine and the law, and into social psychology.

We are back again to this problem of social role, and in my second lecture I want to talk about those social organizations—one old, education; and one relatively new, social work—who have other assumptions about the development and nature of personality that may perhaps be more closely related to our modern scientific understanding.

LECTURE II

We must now turn to the other groups who are increasingly involved in the process of trying to improve an individual's functioning in society. There are, firstly, the various types of persons in the social services—Almoners, renamed Medical Social Workers; Psychiatric Social Workers, and Child Care Officers, are examples of some who are losing their individual professional identities in many ways as regards training and organization. We have also to consider school counsellors, and educational and clinical psychologists, who are now interesting themselves actively in treatment, though in order to avoid medical overtones this is delicately re-christened 'Behaviour Modification'.

The rise of the relatively independent profession of social work is an expression of, as well as a stimulus to, our understanding of social processes as they affect human behaviour. It is only comparatively recently that social workers have achieved any corporate identity. The beginnings of social work are enshrined in the genteel lady almoner and the rent collector of the early Housing Trusts. There are also other centres of growth—in the probation service, in the school attendance officer (for me, and for most other people, still inevitably referred to as 'the School Board man'), and in the Children's Officers who grew out of the efforts of voluntary societies' concern with child poverty and cruelty. Again, the term 'cruelty man', like 'School Board man', echoes down from generations past.

A series of great reports—Curtis, Younghusband, and, most recently, Seebohm,[1] have given visible expression to the gradual clarification of generic social work. By this is meant (hopefully perhaps) a system of theory and practice that can be learnt and then applied to a variety of social situations, in much the same way as medicine is a general system of theory and practice which can then be vocationally applied to such disparate fields as mending broken bones or correcting the metabolic changes produced by kidney disease. Medicine started as a whole and is now fragmented;[2] social work had disparate origins and is now unifying.

For the most part, social workers have had to do much of their own training, even at a theoretical level. Academics in psychology and sociology usually look down their noses at this applied and practical stuff, even more than pure scientists averting their eyes from the grubby practicalities of physicians' training, to the

[1] Kathleen Woodroofe, *From Charity to Social Work* (Toronto, 1962).

[2] Some evidence of this at first surprising statement is called for. For years teachers of medicine have realized that students on qualification are not competent to practise any, let alone most, branches of medicine, without further specialist training (even for general practice), a fact now recognized by the General Medical Council. The idea of a shorter 'core curriculum' and then longer vocational training is gaining ground, so that there may soon be little common language and practice between, for example, a psychiatrist and a physician who is a specialist in kidney disease. On the organizational side there is a proliferation of Royal Colleges of this and that (Pathology and Psychiatry are the latest) so that it is possible for Government and society to divide and rule in a way that was unlikely when just the Royal Colleges of Physicians and Surgeons represented the higher [*sic!*] medical establishment. On the laboratory research side the initiatives are now firmly with non-medical scientists like biochemists. Lastly, it will already be seen that one theme of these lectures is the shift of emphasis from the medical to the social and psychological in the management of human problems.

benefit of neither side. One might perhaps note in passing that physicists and chemists long ago gave up their inhibitions about sharing with practical engineers. Perhaps the sciences which are least sure of their academic status are understandably the most hesitant to dabble in trade or, even worse, in political and social issues that might raise passions.

The contrasting humanist and scientific approaches to sociology have, of course, been actively, and often acidly, debated ever since Comte's day. The problem is in principle somewhat different from that which has always concerned physicians who, not infrequently, find some sort of conflict between their purely scientific, investigatory interests and their overriding concern for patients. But the errors against which physicians struggle are diseases caused by foreign organisms or biological processes, whereas the sociology student and social worker almost by definition see the problems they study as caused by men and men only. Hence the need to steer between scientific objectivity and a proper care for human beings can cause double vision and resulting confusion of role.

As I write these lectures, directors of social work for towns and counties all over the country are being appointed. This is the outward, visible and convincing expression of the coming of age of social work as an activity that does not need to go on under anybody's umbrella, like that of medicine, as in medical or psychiatric social work; or the law, as in the probation service or the statutory activities of Children's Departments. The emergence of social workers as an independent profession means that for the first time a new, wholly secular organization with codified theory and practice is becoming primarily responsible for human misfits, inadequacies, and miseries.

The idea that social workers are dealing with personal problems rather than social difficulties is perhaps unfamiliar to many of their clients, and even sometimes to their medical colleagues. In hospital service the lady almoner was originally envisaged as the provider of some of the basic material necessities of the deserving poor in order that these deficiencies would not hinder the doctor's healing role. The arrival of the welfare state has relieved her of much of this type of welfare work, but there are still many such roles at a more sophisticated level; for example, guiding a client through the bureaucratic maze to the welfare provisions to which he or she may be entitled.

The Child Care Officer is also now much more a family-centred man or woman, less concerned with physical neglect and cruelty, although these still occur surprisingly and sadly often in our society. Child Care Officers are more interested in the psychological health of those with whom they have to deal, and the inadequacies in this regard of many homes and orphanages is now a matter of public concern.

Probation Officers have always had a rather more critical role but, though their clients often still perceive them as 'coppers in mufti', their training and philosophy is now directed towards understanding the adult and adolescent criminal mind. They provide a bridge between family and society that so many children coming from broken homes need when on probation. They also give much marriage guidance for couples who come ostensibly about separation or maintenance orders, or other legal matters.

All such workers are now trained to see that, behind the demand for some immediate satisfaction of apparent social needs, such as rehousing, there may be a human or family problem that should be tackled as well. Then the demands for material help may be made—and met—more realistically. Being no longer the handmaidens (or handymen) of those who had seemed their elders and betters in the ancient professions has led social workers to examine their roles anew. However, their client-centred, usually supportive function, cannot be their only way of working. This has always laid them open to the Marxist critique that they adjust men and women to society without questioning society's values. They do not try to influence the social structure that seems so often to have aggravated, if not caused, the conditions for which their clients seek help, be it delinquency or neurosis. In a thoughtful article, Dame Eileen Younghusband[1] says that social workers must take more part in social planning and therefore in moral values. Power is being thrust upon them because of their special knowledge of family and social interactions. They could and should be involved in decisions about priorities when resources are limited; for example, the Housing Department might have a different view of eviction from the Social Service Department. In some respects, of course, their problems are similar to those which doctors have always had to face.

[1] Dame Eileen Younghusband, 'Social Work and Social Values in Social Work Today' in *Journal of the British Association of Social Workers*, vol. 1, no. 6, Sept. 1970, p. 5.

A patient has a right to refuse treatment and compulsory hospitalization is only used to protect others and himself from the probable fatal consequences of his refusal. In social-work practice the right of self-determination is the traditional safeguard against social workers being used as agents of conformity. However, I quote Dame Eileen Younghusband:

> This principle is shot at nowadays as a manifestation of an individualist philosophy which takes too little account of the family as a group, of the social milieu and social mores in which people are embedded, and the effect which cultural values have on people's perceptions and decisions. It also assumes a rational self which knows what it wants and won't be happy till it gets it. In practice, the trouble with many of the clients of social workers is that they are ambivalent, torn with conflict, immature, inadequate, apt to project their troubles or aggression on to other people, so that what they want may bear little relation to reality. Who or what then is the self that determines? This problem becomes even more difficult in family therapy, or work with groups or communities. Has the concept any real meaning in this context? Or does self-determination mean that what the majority or most powerful individuals decide, they want?

In his description of the Personal Service Professions to which I have already referred in my first lecture, Professor Halmos[1] says that they have been influenced by what he calls the counselling ideology, which has three values:

(*a*) Abandonment of judgement and condemnation coupled with humility and stoical acceptance;

[1] Paul Halmos, *The Personal Service Society*, p. 19.

(*b*) Cultivation of a mutually honest and intimate I-and-Thou relationship between man and man;

(*c*) The war on humbug, self-deception, false righteousness, anger, and idolatries.

As he says, such an ideology has strong Christian and Hippocratic undertones. It is also of interest to compare these remarks with Karl Mannheim's comments,[1] made some years before in the early 1930s, on the decline of the spiritual elements, utopian as well as ideological, in modern society: 'It is possible that the best that our ethical principles have to offer is genuineness and frankness in place of the old ideals.' He does, however, go on to make the point, 'Have we reached the stage where we can dispense with strivings? Would not this elimination of all tension be also the elimination of political activity, scientific zeal—in fact, the very content of life itself?'

But though the underlying philosophy of counselling may go far back into the history of our society, the dominating theories guiding everyday practices of counsellors largely originate in Freud's work and are no more than half a century old. It would take too long to describe the relevant essential features of Freudian psychology, and in any case psychoanalytic concepts are part of every intellectual's stock-in-trade these days, though precious little good that does them when they get into the usual emotional crises and interpersonal difficulties of daily living.

Freud's clinical orientation as a medical doctor has influenced society's attitudes to all sorts of behaviour,

[1] Karl Mannheim, *Ideology and Utopia* (Kegan Paul, London, 1946), p. 231.

normal and abnormal. His pervasive influence is well set out by Philip Rieff, in his aptly titled book, *The Triumph of the Therapeutic.*[1] It would also be quite wrong to imagine that Freudian psychology in theory and practice is a fixed revelation unchanging and unchangeable. The insights which Freudian psychology has given into many diverse fields, such as art, anthropology, and religion are complemented by the changes wrought in the dynamic psychologies by contacts with other sciences and observers of human nature. There are, in addition, the changes made by further clinical studies by analysts themselves.

In spite of all their theoretical impurities,[2] dynamic psychologies have provided until recently virtually the only comprehensive and workable basis to understanding and influencing human interactions and behaviour. The reasons for this dominance are various, and I can only mention two. The first is the fact that the actual language of dynamic psychology can be joined on to that of everyday experience. Thus client and counsellor can speak to one another in a way that they could never do with an esoteric scientific language of personality types and psychological test scores.

The second is that dynamic theory alone provides a fairly comprehensive understanding of the central

[1] Philip Rieff, *The Triumph of the Therapeutic* (Chatto & Windus, London, 1966).

[2] One insuperable theoretical difficulty is the impossibility of unifying any theory that assumes the reality of psychic energy with all non-dynamic psychological theories of human personality. Biologists have properly abandoned all vitalist theories years ago—even physical energy is recognized to be a theoretical construct rather than a measurable fact. Possible ways out of the theoretical impasse are too complex to describe, and in any case are irrelevant to the themes of these lectures.

situation of counselling, namely the confrontation between client and counsellor—an I–Thou situation—a meeting which is far more fraught with emotional tensions than the polite word 'interview' might suggest. The concentration of present-day psychological theories, both dynamic and non-dynamic, on the here-and-now situations of one-to-one confrontations and small group situations is one of the most interesting and important recent developments in psychology.

Many people have, of course, always been intuitively very good at understanding the unspoken significance of meetings that they have with people, whether professionally or not. It is this type of person who, with comparatively little training, seems to be able to be quite effective in certain forms of counselling; for example, marriage guidance. There is a tendency to stratify various types of counselling. Some appear comparatively superficial and easy; for example a social worker's interview mainly on a welfare problem. Others appear so deep and complicated that only a medically qualified psychotherapist is supposed to be able to conduct such treatment, though the medical contribution could be no more than 'magic'. What is really meant is that the more experienced and well-trained therapist can manage a wider range of situations and types of behaviour found in his clients. He is able to understand the hidden meanings of apparently quite incomprehensible word associations or gestures, and can carry the emotional burden of being in part responsible for his patients' anti-social or self-destructive impulses. Even the most experienced therapist, however, has his blind spots, and at all levels the continued opportunity for counsellors to discuss what is going on between themselves and their clients, is necessary for all.

The social situations in which client and counsellor can practise under the ideological values that I have already quoted from Halmos, are many and various. What they share in common is a need to operate in a social situation that allows their relationships to be varied according to the needs of the client, and in ways that these can be explicitly spelled out. In particular, the rigid hierarchical situation of authority figure, be it doctor, teacher, or prison officer, is incompatible with the full possibility of using the I–Thou relationship in treatment. The open prison, the unlocked ward—even a lack of school uniform and a permissive, creative class atmosphere—point to the less structured social-group situations that are now becoming commonplace. There are unsolved problems in the nature of the appropriate constraints in all such groups, even in purely therapeutic groups.

It is important to note that unstructured does not mean undisciplined. Individual psychotherapy means nearly always that the client has a regular time to attend. The couch is commonly used to encourage the relaxation necessary for deep therapy; namely, the uncensored free association technique. For group and individual treatment clients must be there, and the reasons for non-attendance are often usefully and minutely analysed to show up the nature of resistance to treatment. Psychotherapy is emphatically not walk-in, on-demand feeding, though at times within the analytical hour patients may be very regressed indeed in their behaviour.

We may now turn to consider a still more recent member of the counselling professions—the school counsellor. Parallel to the rise of social work as an independent organization connected with disturbances of adult behaviour, is the rise of the concept of child development as something closely connected with, but perhaps distinct from, the ordinary process of education. For many people even today, education is seen just as a process of knocking hard facts into unwilling blockheads; i.e. something purely 'adaptive'. The courses of study prescribed are regulated from outside the child, usually epitomized by Examination Boards' syllabuses. They may have greater or less relevance to the social roles the child will later be expected to perform.

But there is also a thin line of educational reformers from Pestalozzi and Montessori to A. S. Neill[1] who have seen the child not as a passive recipient of what society thought was good for it, but as a potential human being with qualities and capacities that need to be encouraged to grow, rather than forced into a pre-set mould. In addition to this realization that those who are being taught are by no means uniform, there has been a growing realization that the mould being prepared for them by society may itself be influenced by parents and not just political philosophy. Again we see that the apparent relative autonomy of a profession (in this case teaching) has to give way to the realization of its role in society as in the case of medicine and law. Just as the physician now has his colleagues, the social workers, so also we see the teacher more or less willingly

[1] For example, William Body, *The History of Western Education* (Adam & Charles Black, London, 9th edn., 1969).

collaborating with the educational psychologist and, more recently, with the school counsellor, and with the medically orientated child psychiatry clinic not far away.

The good teacher has, of course, always done counselling, though I doubt if many of them ever thought of their personal interest in, and concern for, some pupils in these terms, and would be as surprised at this concept as M. Jourdain was that he spoke in prose all the time. I am sure all of us have been indebted as a child to perhaps one or two teachers whose personal influence far outweighed their strictly professional role as purveyors of knowledge and ideas.

In a recent symposium[1] Maurice Craft relates the growth of this comparatively new activity in schools to three factors. Firstly, the post-war egalitarian political ideology which means that more children have more education with more attention paid to see that they profit by it. Secondly, the advances in an industrial society produce more uncertainty about the future roles youngsters will have. In eras of rapid social change, social mobility, and decline in the power of authority of the family, a child needs someone to give him or her guidance. Lastly, society needs more and more people with more and more training. Despite the general impression, figures suggest that the shortage is greater of those with higher education rather than of those who are 'hewers of wood and drawers of water'.

This last point in particular again raises the question of whether guidance and counselling is for the benefit of the individual primarily, or the state. Education, much

[1] H. Lytton and M. Craft (ed.), *Guidance and Counselling in British Schools* (Arnold, London, 1969).

more than medicine, and perhaps even more than the law, is quite clearly an instrument for conveying society's philosophy to the young. However, it is assumed (at any rate in most Western countries) that the educational processes also teach the capacity to form independent judgements. It is more than half recognized that a society of sheep is unlikely to throw up the responsible and responsive leaders that are needed. It will favour those that can reach the top only by cunning and violence and not merit.

The activities of the school counsellor are apparent in three main fields; firstly, educational guidance in the sense of what are the best courses for the child to pursue; secondly, vocational guidance of what sort of things would be best for the child to do on leaving school (sometimes this is already done by a Careers Master); and thirdly, and less clearly, personal counselling. This last role, of course, borders on to the whole area of child psychotherapy and child guidance. The interactions in a child between emotional difficulties and educational problems are complex and often unclear. Furthermore, the modes of tackling it differ widely according to the theory of the counsellor. To judge by Lytton and Craft's symposium, school counselling is seen as entirely child-orientated. Parents are scarcely involved at all. This is in contrast to much contemporary thinking in child psychiatry where, as already mentioned, the whole emphasis is on the child's disturbance being largely the product of disturbed family relationships. This carries the corollary that management of the latter may be more successful than direct attention to the child.

It must be admitted, however, that there is no hard evidence at all about the relative efficacy of any particular method of treatment in child psychiatry, or indeed of most 'therapies' in psychiatry. Therapeutic uncertainty, however, should not blind us to the fact that there is now a good deal of clinical evidence, including direct observational studies, of family interactions producing children's disturbances. This is particularly true of the pre-school child, which is the period of life that is more and more becoming the focus of interest, not only for psychologists, but also for educationalists and those concerned with social welfare. The Plowden Report is an eloquent expression of this new concern with the early stages of child development.

There is thus much of value in contemporary research into here-and-now situations in which counselling occurs. However, as I said at the beginning of my first lecture, this series is about Beginnings, Ends, and Means, and if we are to discuss the possibilities of preventing psychological disorders developing, then we do have to go back to looking at the development of human personality as one can see it in the family setting.

It does not need modern psychological knowledge to convince people that the child is father of the man. What the newer knowledge can do is to help us understand more clearly how early influences, especially those in the home, profoundly affect adult attitudes and patterns of behaviour. Much adult fantasy has gone into describing what the intrinsic nature of man is at birth, usually resulting in a splendid confusion of origin and essence. Doctrines of original sin have on the whole exerted a malign influence on adult attitudes to childish misbehaviour. The inevitable reactions, especially in the Age of Reason, resulted in equally unlikely doctrines of original innocence, such as those propounded by Rousseau. These in turn have degenerated into the total permissiveness in upbringing that was fashionable in some circles not so long ago. It probably had as pernicious an effect on the unfortunate child victims as the harsh repressiveness of older generations.

In the last hundred years or so, study of the child in his or her own right has gradually come about in literal as well as in scientific circles. Coveney's book[1] gives an interesting account of the changing attitudes of novelists and playwrights to children. Visual artists' interest in the child's view of the world as a source of inspiration did not come till later. Society's concern for the welfare of children does not follow an exactly parallel course. Pinchbeck and Hewitt,[2] for example, in their study of the history of child care in England regard the legislation of Tudor times as being comparatively enlightened and genuinely concerned with the social welfare of vagrant and orphaned children as well as the education of the offspring of all classes, not just those of the rich. The eighteenth and early nineteenth centuries seemed to show less concern, though at all times children were regarded as 'little adults', to be pushed into all adult roles as soon as practicable. (Books and clothing specifically for children were scarcely thought of till the end of the eighteenth century.) Of course, the apparent brutality of child care has to be seen against

[1] Peter Coveney, *The Image of Childhood* (Penguin Books, Harmondsworth, 1967).

[2] Ivy Pinchbeck and M. Hewitt, *Children in English Society* (Routledge & Kegan Paul, London, 1969).

the background of vast infant mortality, the commonplace of early death of all ages of childhood and young adult life, and the presence of unrelievable disease and pain almost universally. Nowadays we have, as it were, the psychological space and time to look at childhood, then a prolonged adult life, and finally healthy old age. We no longer need to sow much seed in order to have a few healthy plants, but can, by taking care and thought, get more nearly what we want in quantity and quality.

However, the scientific investigation of child development needs a particular degree of objectivity that is, perhaps, harder to acquire than the objective study of the phenomena of nature remote from man himself. From the scientific point of view, we cannot yet say with any certainty what exact functions in feeling, perception, and learning are already active at birth. We can be sure, however, that the child's mind is not a *tabula rasa* on which can be moulded any behaviour pattern whatsoever. As a physician, one knows that there are many physical factors that enter into the limitation of a child's potentiality. Everyone recognizes the gross and obvious ones, like congenital malformation leading to mental abnormality. The extent to which minor subnormalities in the brain may produce minor psychological effects is, however, a matter of great controversy. In any case, the malign effects of physical disorders of the brain acquired through difficulties *in utero* or at birth will probably diminish, and even disappear, as our understanding increases of the optimum conditions for early development.

The genetic influences on personality growth have

unfortunately been the subject of some flesh-creeping science-fiction type of writing. Genetic engineering is a theoretical probability within the next few years, so that at any rate the sex of babies may be decided at will, if not other characteristics. I do not think, however, that these possibilities pose any problems fundamentally different from those which we are now considering in discussing mainly the environmental psychological influences on child behaviour; they simply put back the matter of choice to an earlier stage. The outstanding characteristic of the human newborn is its relative immaturity physiologically, so that an immense amount of post-natal development occurs mainly under the influence of environmental and therefore manipulable factors.

The study of child development has shown the greatest clash between the two most fertile, articulate, and influential types of psychological theory—those so-called psychodynamic ones that ultimately originate in Freud, and the behaviouristic ones whose parentage is more mixed, so that no single name, except perhaps that of Pavlov, can be evoked as their progenitor.

There are many different ways in which one can characterize differences between these two types of theory. For my purpose, one of the most useful is by making use of a familiar dichotomy in psychological theory and practice between expressive and adaptive society.[1] Much developmental psychology seems to be concerned with adaptive behaviour in the sense of learning to do an activity, such as driving a car, solving

[1] G. Allport and P. E. Vernon, *Studies in Expressive Movement* (Macmillan, London, 1933).

a sum, and even something as complex as bringing up a child. On the other side, there are psychologists who are interested in finding the way a man expresses his personality—the life style—in the particular ways he does these activities. The psychological necessity for self-expression somehow and somewhere needs no emphasis—we are not human if just automata, but in our society there are more and more activities which leave no room for self-expression: car-driving is such a one!

It is the great merit of the psychodynamic school that it has been able to give a coherent account of the self-expressive aspects of behaviour, especially the ways in which bodily activities and sensations are linked to primitive emotion and continue to exert their directive power on seemingly well-adapted adult behaviour. The human mind seems to have a capacity to leave islands of primitive thinking, emotion, and behaviour, buried in the adult personality, that may suddenly erupt and take over even the best-controlled adult mind, resulting in disordered outbursts in ways that are described differently according to the form and situation of occurrence. In one context they may appear as symptoms, bodily disturbances, depression, etc.; or in another context there may seem to be antisocial behaviour, such as compulsive stealing. In the third, the behaviour may seem to be neither ill nor criminal, but carelessly indifferent to hitherto more or less satisfactory adult human relationships in, for example, a marriage. The protean nature of these manifestations of a disturbance in development, make it difficult to find a satisfactory vocabulary to accommodate them all, save technical psychological terms.

However, as well as often having detrimental effects, these islands of immaturity are essential growth points enabling adults to make new and more constructive adaptations when faced with difficult life crises. This is more important from the theoretical point of view and accords with Jung's ideas on the creative aspects of a neurotic illness in ordinary people. What may appear to be a regression in behaviour and thinking during psychotherapy is often a temporary return to an old pattern of adaptation in order to restructure it—a psychic parallel of 'reculer pour mieux sauter'.

Too close an analogy between mental and physical diseases can be made when discussing psychoprophylaxis. There is a large factor of cultural relativity involved in drawing arbitrary lines between normal and abnormal, law-abiding and criminal. However, the whole gamut of psychological reaction types has been described in many different societies, strongly suggesting that there are common underlying biological factors influencing their appearance whatever the cultural factors influencing their precipitation. But too great an emphasis on the psychic determinism that the influence of the biological factors suggests, results only too often in the sufferer regarding himself as the victim of a 'medical disorder' or constitutional imbalance for which he cannot be held in any way responsible. The influence of such an idea is shown, for example, in concepts, such as diminished responsibility, that cause such difficulties in medico-legal cases.

Many psychologists, but particularly those of the psychodynamic school, stress the extent to which the personality of the parent, and later that of the teacher, affects the way in which a child is capable of learning even an apparently purely mechanical activity. There is an important sense in which the child's personality is at first its mother's personality—seeing the world as dangerous or as gratifying precisely to the extent that mother sees it as dangerous or gratifying. The baby only slowly becomes separate from the mother and tends to learn in proportion to the extent to which it can identify with other adults; for example, taking over, at first uncritically and unconsciously, their ways of perception, thought, and behaviour. Such a process cannot easily be expressed in other terms such as conditioning, or even imprinting, which, in any case are somewhat doubtful psychological explanations.

The identification with a parent figure means that the child often becomes the vehicle of the parent's own feelings; a point of great importance in expressive psychology which can become too individualistic. This can be particularly true for feelings that the parent herself (or himself) cannot express openly. Some of the exciting present advances in developmental psychology have been in our understanding of the subtle interactions between child, mother, father, and sibs, which carry enormous implications for child care, and indeed the whole educational structure, not to mention us poor parents who, as young mothers and fathers, might never have started if we had realized what was coming to us.

To round out the picture of new approaches to changing human behaviour, I should say something briefly about the rise of behaviour therapy in the 1960s. This is essentially an application of various types of learning theory as formulated by psychologists for the cure of psychiatric symptoms, such as phobias, compulsions, perversions. The basic hypothesis behind this approach is that psychiatric disorder, especially neurotic behaviour, is learned, maladapted behaviour which should be unlearned and replaced by more socially adapted patterns of behaviour. Various techniques are used, involving applications of the general principles of reward for good—that is, adapted—and punishment for bad—that is, maladapted behaviour, respectively. Most people would regard the approach as somewhat crude and mechanical, but there is clear evidence that with certain types of patients undoubted more or less permanent relief from symptoms can be obtained, even when other methods have failed.[1]

By way of illustrating the contrast between this approach and more orthodox methods of trying to change people's behaviour, it is instructive to look at punishment as opposed to aversion therapy. In the latter, for example, a patient may receive mild electric shocks, or other painful stimuli, to condition an avoidance reaction to stimuli or situations (for example, perverse sexual images). Subjects come voluntarily for aversion therapy, and the person who administers the treatment is essentially impersonal. Whether or not a legal rule has been broken is immaterial, and the whole aim of the treatment is forward looking. In contrast, punishment may be meted out to a prisoner whether or not he wishes it, and the relationship between the victim, society generally, and the particular people (for example,

[1] V. Meyer and E. Chesser, *Behaviour Therapy in Clinical Psychiatry* (Penguin Books, Harmondsworth, 1970).

the personnel of the prison service) who administer it is clearly loaded with all sorts of emotions. Punishment is also seen as something retributive as well as deterrent or reformatory. Thus, punishment may have some elements of aversion therapy in it, but not vice versa.

An excellent example of the application of rewards for 'good behaviour' as opposed to punishment for bad behaviour has just been published by that arch-behaviourist, Bertram Skinner.[1] It is particularly relevant to these lectures as it refers to the treatment of a group of adolescents disturbed in ways similar to those of our patient, William. I quote:

A new social environment was constructed in which no boy was required to do anything. He could sleep on a pad in a dormitory, eat nutritious if not very palatable food, and sit on a bench all day. But he could greatly improve his lot by earning points exchangeable for more delicious food at mealtimes, admission to games-rooms, the rental of a private room or television set, or even a short vacation away from the school. He could earn points by doing simple chores, but much more easily by learning things. Correct responses to programmed instructional materials and correct answers in examinations after studying other kinds of material meant points.

The results were dramatic. Boys who had been convinced by the school system that they were unteachable discovered that they were not. They learned reading and writing and arithmetic, and acquired other verbal and manual skills.

[1] Bertram F. Skinner, in *The Listener*, 30 Sept. 1971, p. 431. He is quoting from studies of Dr. Harold Cohen and colleagues at the Institute of Behaviour Research, Washington, D.C.

They did so without compulsion, and the hostile behaviour characteristic of such institutions quickly disappeared.

Skinner, however, is an honest and serious scientist and points out that the success rate was still poor—in fact nearly half the boys had relapsed within one year of leaving this special community (the usual figure would have been nearer 100 per cent). Within a few years back in 'ordinary' society, the boys could hardly be distinguished from the rest of the delinquent culture in which they had been brought up and to which they had returned.

It is too early to say how widely applicable learning theories may be to modification of human behaviour, but I suspect that it will always have a modest place, which has certainly to be taken into account when one considers the full range of possible new techniques that societies may have for modifying human behaviour.

A thorough and systematic application of the various psychosocial techniques available for modifying human behaviour has implications for the organization of a national psychosocial service that would in part pre-empt some of the roles of the traditional professions, especially medicine and law. With the increasing sophistication of knowledge about human personality development, it could be that many who now turn to the doctor for psychological aid, with or without presenting somatic symptoms, will go elsewhere, leaving the doctor free to concentrate on his special knowledge of how the body works and its contribution to mental development and disorder. It is possible that this will result in an inversion of the present positions of medicine and the counselling professions, with the latter in control of the former rather than vice versa. The doctor may become a superior somatic technician, and no longer necessarily the leader of the therapeutic team.

As far as the law is concerned, legal processes are still rightly needed to determine matters of fact—did the accused commit the crime or not? What to do with the law-breaker once this is proven is a complex technical matter, probably best left to a special branch of the counselling professions.

The delay in this reversal of roles is, of course, partly the result of the conservatism of society generally, and the reluctance of people to put their trust in new authority figures. Their scepticism is fully justified, since we cannot claim that counselling professions have even part of some of the answers, but the trend is there, and will continue. The theoretical weaknesses of counselling professions are, however, immense, as we have seen in our brief survey of social work, school counselling, and behaviour modification by learning theories. The practical weaknesses of the quality and quantity of the counselling personnel are even greater. Similar logistic difficulties were found in the teaching professions when compulsory education was introduced one hundred years ago, and somehow they were slowly overcome—so we can take heart.

In the field of counselling, group work is comparatively new; in fact, it has almost entirely developed since the Second World War.[1] Like so many original

[1] S. H. Foulkes and E. J. Anthony, *Group Psychotherapy* (Penguin Books, Harmondsworth, 1957), gives a good general account of the history and theory of group psychotherapy.

ideas, it was born partly out of sheer necessity—namely, the need of army psychiatrists to treat large numbers of soldiers with inadequate resources of personnel and time. But the originators quickly and imaginatively seized on the implications and began to study the social structures of small groups intensively and in their own right, from which we have learnt a great deal about the complex interactions of people in such situations. Much of this knowledge, of course, merely formalizes what has always been known intuitively by good managers of men, and, in a more sinister way, by the unscrupulous politician. Originally, the therapeutic group was relatively small and close, but the general ideas underlying such groups have now been extended into the therapeutic community involving the functioning of whole wards and even psychiatric hospitals. These ideas have revolutionized the care of the severely mentally ill and are beginning also to penetrate more widely into psychiatry, and even beyond that, into general areas where group psychology is relevant—for example, industrial management. We have here an important example of a whole new area of knowledge which owes little or nothing to the traditional ways of medicine, law, and education.

Let us now return to the patient, William, and see if the newer approaches get us any further in understanding and managing his problems. In the first place we are driven straight away to ask more about his early development and family milieu. Might there be some genetic instability that rendered him less amenable to the ordinary processes of upbringing in the family? This refers to the general question of the somatic constitutional contribution to personality unrelated to these lectures.

To what extent are the problems now showing themselves in adolescence reflecting the parents' own uncertainties in their adult roles? To go deeply into this would require more knowledge of the parents' personalities than I have, since the opportunity to explore the family dynamics has not arisen. We do know, however, that William's father is himself going through a crisis in relationship to his own work pattern. There are also signs of tension between mother and father. I suspect that both of them are content, subconsciously, to have William as a scapegoat acting out all the madness of the family on their behalf. The here-and-now formulation of parent/child interactions is in general much more useful for the young patient than too great a concentration on the parents' own difficulties which in turn obviously stem from their own upbringing. One could go backwards in this cycle all the way to Adam and Eve—and we all know what a mess they made of bringing up Cain and Abel!

Let us now turn to the social aspects of William's condition and see if it is helpful to try and look at the world and himself as he sees it. There are a multiplicity of ways of life, some hedonistic, others puritanical, which are offered to him by the mass media and personal contact as if in a sort of psychic supermarket, all differently priced and packaged. It is hardly surprising that his crisis of identity should be so stormy, and that special arrangements outside the family were needed to help him. The school to which he was sent is strongly oriented to personal counselling, and the relationship he developed with the rather special kind of school counselling it provides has given him an opportunity to find himself.

I should like to conclude by describing my private Freudo-Marxist Utopia-Hell. Much of it derives from Aldous Huxley's *Brave New World*, and Bertram Skinner's *Walden Two*[1]—the latter has had, on the whole, surprisingly little impact, particularly on this side of the Atlantic. In *Utopia and its Enemies*,[2] George Kateb describes the three essential elements of all Utopias as being the preservation of perpetual peace, guaranteed abundance of the physical necessities of life, and conditioned virtue. Of the first two attributes I have nothing to say, since these conditions depend for their creation on political strategies and technological skills, of which I have no special knowledge. The concept of conditioned virtue is, however, central to these lectures. Kateb's discussion of it revolves mainly around objections to Skinner's *Walden Two*, which was published in 1948 when it must have seemed astonishingly *avant-garde*. It was an attempt to take seriously the application of conditioning principles to early childhood development so that, at least in theory, the ideals of the community would be automatically and joyfully followed without any sense of strain or non-conformity in the personality. As symbolized in the title, Skinner's book is in the mainstream of Utopia writing, which was, in the nineteenth century, chiefly American. Moreover, it was mainly in that large and free country that some of these

[1] B. F. Skinner, *Walden Two* (Macmillan, London, 1948).

[2] George Kateb, *Utopia and its Enemies* (Free Press of Glencoe: Collier-Macmillan, New York, 1963).

ideas could be realized, at any rate temporarily, in more or less self-governing communities that sprang up in large numbers all over the country.

Some of the objections to such Utopias centre on the idea that personality is entirely knowable, so there is nothing mysterious in man which cannot be understood and therefore controlled. Secondly, many feel some distaste for the idea that man can become effortlessly moral. It offends the puritanical idea of many Western societies that goodness must imply effort and suffering. Thirdly, and perhaps most importantly, a Utopia seems to imply *final* perfection with no further development being either necessary or possible, so history will stand still and all men be complacently happy with their role in life. To be fair to Skinner, one must say that he does recognize this limitation, but has no clear answer to it.

My gloss on *Walden Two* concerns the nature of the rewards for work and conforming behaviour. In a state of guaranteed abundance, rewards based on earning money are irrelevant, since everything can, in theory, be available for everyone. A limiting factor has to be built in early in personality development, so that men and women will be satisfied with the housing and provisions that the current state of technology could provide. Hoarding and greed—primitive pre-genital aspects of personality—would thus not be positively encouraged by society and rewards would be more in terms of increased opportunities for sexuality in its recreational rather than procreational function.

Of course, all Utopias, including Skinner's, eliminate the family as it has been known for centuries in

Western society. It is worth noting that compulsory education was introduced in the nineteenth century in the face of considerable opposition from the majority of people on many grounds, of which this was just one—namely, that universal state education would undermine the traditional authority of the family.

In the end the logical implications of psychoprophylaxis lead to compulsory child guidance, or, better, compulsory family guidance in the broadest sense. Parenthood might become a status acquired by competitive examination like membership of the House of Lords in Iolanthe. An early nineteenth-century French educational theorist coined the term Orthophrenia,[1] i.e. straight mind. A State Institute of Orthophrenia, charged with the duty of issuing certificates of parenthood, seems to me perfectly to express the final horror of a Freudo-Marxist Utopia-Hell. A way out of this impasse is, I think, to look again at counselling, which depends more on expressive than adaptive aspects of personality, and this will be the topic of the third lecture.

[1] I am indebted to Dr. Alexander Walk for this reference. See his 'Pre-history of Child Psychiatry', *Brit. J. Psychiat.* 1964, 110, 754.

LECTURE III

The theme of these lectures seems so far to lead us to that Big Brother concept of the State that, as foretold by George Orwell, might be here by 1984—only thirteen unlucky years ahead. In this third lecture I hope we can find a partial answer to the impasse by looking more closely at the nature of the counselling process in individual and group situations. This gives us a more creative—and I believe more religious—view of ourselves, and thus may re-establish man's position against the State. If a change does not occur, then I think damnation is not too strong a word for our fate.

I want to start with an apparently oblique approach by asking the question, Who should pay for personal counselling? In Roman times, persons exercising the so-called liberal arts, such as philosophers, advocates, teachers, physicians, received no fees, as such arts would be debased by appearing to be provided as a hired service. This lordly disdain of money was fine as long as there were slaves to do the work, but of necessity the State now has to provide in one way or another for all such practitioners—even philosophers. However, if the State pays the piper, it will call the tune, and the possible dangers of this can be seen in several ways; for example, the National Health Service functions more or less as long as the doctor, the patient, and the State agree on when and how a person is ill and what sort of treatment is best. Difficulties arise when they disagree, of which current examples are therapeutic abortion, contraception, and, to a certain extent, mental health. Sometimes it is conservative doctors who are reluctant to implement what public opinion, as filtered through Parliament to the Health Department, clearly expects. At other times State organizations are reluctant to implement some unpopular recommendations from medical and allied professionals (for example, on the subjects of smoking, or fluoridation). Professional organizations independent of the State certainly help to preserve some freedom of action for their members. In the case of medicine, one can instance the complementary but very different function of the General Medical Council and the British Medical Association. These organizations are often the target of brickbats, but their value is more apparent when one looks at the state of medicine in countries where such organizations are absent or weak. However, such organizations are themselves, of course, open at least to a class bias, as Marxists and others are never tired of pointing out. The risk of professionals being on the side of the State against the individual is probably increased when the profession is wholly paid directly from the centre.

There are also some problems to consider about the ways in which people should pay for personal counselling (as opposed to the problem of how the counsellors get paid). In the main, we seem to have got accustomed to the idea that compulsory direct taxation is the best way of extracting money for essential national services, though the administrative machinery whereby this is done obviously varies enormously from country to country. In the case of counselling there is still, however, a large private sector not only in the narrow sense of people paying for individual psychotherapy from medical and non-medical qualified psychotherapists, but also in the centuries-old tradition of alms-giving for the support of the clergy. One can perhaps go even further than this, echoing an idea first put forward by George Bernard Shaw. Michael Kustow, former Director of the Institute of Contemporary Arts, said recently that experimental small theatres were social therapy and should be financed by the Minister of Social Security! The difficulty about indirect methods of payment is that in this way the implications of psychological difficulties may get lost. There is a time in some people's lives when there is an apparent inverse relationship between welfare needs and psychological problems. This is not to say that the world is full of psychopathic shirkers who are making indefinite demands on the welfare services when they should instead be supporting themselves. It is more common as a phase of treatment which has to be worked through when the client may not at all accept the implications of personal responsibility to which the counsellor is directing him. Financial responsibility is perhaps the most potent way of bringing home the implications of responsibility, and all I am suggesting is that this element is often left out in political and economic arguments about ways of financing services for the community. Money is power and we ignore the subtleties of its effects on client/professional and professional/State relations at our peril.[1] The greatest difficulties come about when it is a whole family, or even perhaps a whole community, and not the individual, who needs the help—financial and psychological.

Departments of Social Welfare may take over functions and provide help for many conditions now regarded as due to mental illness and therefore by little more than verbal analogy in the province of the Department of Health. Nevertheless, an understanding of the complexities of interpersonal relationships between client and professional in medicine, law, and education, must remain an integral part of training in these disciplines. As long as men have bodies and minds joined together, doctors will have to go on dealing with their reciprocal interactions. As long as there are human beings to educate other human beings, teachers will have to be aware of their personal roles. As long as men and women have to work and think and use the things of this world, they will continue to use them for their own ends and need the law to regulate their conduct.

There is also the problem of the possibility of 'buck-passing' between one department and another; for example, many may rightly feel that the Department of Health ought not to be responsible for those who are merely unhappy or ineffectual, and not physically ill, but these conditions should be the concern of society. At the least, such people can exert a malignant influence on their children, possibly rendering them un-

[1] Richard Titmuss, *Gift Relationship: From Human Blood to Social Policy* (Allen & Unwin, 1971); David Holt, 'Money, Breakdown and Society' (*The Twentieth Century*, 1968–9). In different ways both of these writers challenge currently accepted ideas on paying for health.

able to fulfil themselves as completely as they should; thus, the child may be predisposed not only to delinquency and antisocial behaviour, but also to more illness and a degree of invalidism.

In medicine we are accustomed to the idea (admittedly only after long heart-searching) that patients who are a public health menace but refuse treatment, can be compulsorily treated. However, we rather strictly confine the certification of mentally ill people to those who are a danger to themselves or others. For how long can we afford not to intervene in family situations where we see children being brought up in ways which will inevitably stunt or distort their qualities? The new Children's Act gives wide powers to social workers and the courts, but the most malignant parent/child reactions probably occur at early ages, without producing the overt physical neglect that enables them to act. Neither the parents nor the children may be in a position to ask for help, nor even perceive the need for it. Furthermore, most of us are reluctant to interfere, perhaps being afraid that the beam in our own eye as parents disqualifies us.

The interrelation between profession and society can be usefully regarded as going on at two levels—a conscious one, and a deeper, largely unconscious one which is difficult to describe except indirectly. Everyone recognizes the sense in which the law expresses, at the conscious level, the philosophy of society in defining crimes and misdemeanours. In the same way, the nation's educational system is supposed to equip children to function in the society into which they are growing. The philosophy of life put over by the teachers must not deviate too far from that believed by the parents of such children.

At this conscious level there is still a great deal about which to argue, but I am at this point more interested in the ways in which the individual's roles in society also fulfil certain unconscious needs. At the personal level this has, of course, always been recognized by the great dramatists and novelists. The depth and subtlety of the analysis of these interactions is a good measure of the interest and subtlety of biographies of any well-known person. However, less well known and less well understood are the ways in which social organizations, even the professions, can fulfil some largely unconscious needs, not only of those who work in them, but also in those people who are their clients. I am not so much concerned with the comparatively rare and extreme ways in which certain people obviously distort their role in society for unconscious reasons. For example, the clever but infantile and deprived person who may go into one of the personal service professions and distort his function in it to serve his own ends. There is a proper sense in which social organizations must fulfil some unconscious needs as well as play their manifest role, if they are to retain psychological vitality and validity in society. The best approach, however, to our understanding how this happens is through understanding what goes on in the individual psychotherapy or counselling situation.

In an interesting essay, David Holt traces the origin of the word, *hypokrites*, in ancient Greece.[1] The original

[1] David Holt, *Hypokrites and Analyst* (Guild of Pastoral Psychology, Guild Lecture No. 145, May 1968).

meaning of the word was to express a decision, then to explain or expound, especially dreams or oracles. Then it came to mean to speak in dialogue, and act on the stage; and only quite late did it acquire the sense in which the word, 'hypocritical', is now used; namely, playing a false part. Holt says that in analysis we enact a part with the analyst, and thus obtain relief. This is in line with Aristotle's saying, 'Tragedy is an imitation, not of human beings, but of action in life.' The stage figures do not act in order to represent their characters —they include the characters for the sake of the action.[1] This may be regarded as one of the earliest interpersonal theories of behaviour. Of course, the acting out in the analytical situation is within certain strict rules, as indeed it is on the stage. By and large, in neither situation are people expected to be killed, nor is overt bodily sexual reciprocal play between patient and analyst tolerated. The whole 'as-if' situation, yet with some of the appropriate affect, is the *sine qua non* of treatment. (In passing, it might perhaps be noted that the contemporary fashion for stage nudity, if it ends with public copulation—and perhaps murder too—will undoubtedly defeat the personal psychological and social values of the stage which thus will have fallen to the level of the Roman Circus at its worst.)

In general, we know a good deal about the ways of working of the individual analyst with the individual patient, especially when he is adult. It is a quintessential I–Thou situation into which the client enters freely and is able to leave equally freely. Accurate empathy,

[1] Pirandello's *Six Characters in Search of an Author* subtly expounds this theme.

emotional warmth, and non-judgmental acceptance, are some of the terms used to describe the relationship. Nothing can work if there is not absolute confidentiality, which raises problems in group work. The analyst is cast to play many roles in the client's life, and it is probably easier for him to assume many masks if his underlying real personality is to a certain extent unknown to the client.

Communication of thought and feeling is at one remove, by the interpretation in which one may include not only the word, but also inflection and gesture. It is perhaps not too fanciful to see this process at one end of a continuum that at the other is the baby and its mother where communication is totally physical in warmth, touch, smell, and gentle physical movement. Out of these bits the baby creates the Other that is outside, and yet also inside. For the latter, the Jungian term, 'animus' for the woman, and 'anima' for the male, are perhaps more poetically suggestive and true than the neutral Freudian term, 'the unconscious'. The adult can only use the faceless analyst when he can tolerate the realization that what he makes of the therapist is a bit of himself which has to be taken back in again. The adolescent is in the middle of this continuum; he does not need the total physical maternal contact, but he does need to identify his as yet incomplete other half with a real person. This, I suspect, was the essential psychological function of the godparent who acted as the mature adult with whom the adolescent could identify and through whom he could be introduced into the new Christian society that was increasingly separating itself from the decadent Roman world. How this function has now degenerated! Godparents do practically nothing, and even the Prayer Book seems to require them to do little more than make sure that their godchildren are familiar with the Creed and some prayers. In a similar way, the practice of confession has, over the centuries, lost for most people its valuable cathartic significance by becoming dehumanized, encrusted with ritual, and often divorced from spiritual counselling.

For many people the image of counselling seems nearest to that of mother and child, but in recent years father's role in the family, as principal mediator of society's rules, is being recognized. What can go wrong with his function is expounded in Mitscherlich's pessimistic *Society without the Father*.[1] He points out the psychic dangers of the loss of primary relationships with the father that in many ways are as important as relationships with the mother, though occurring a little later. For example, these days few sons see their father actually working at his job. They thus miss not only learning with or from him the techniques of his job, but also they cannot see him relate to his peers, his masters, and his assistants, and learn how to manage these human relationships.

There is, in addition, a second type of fatherlessness in our society when 'no identifiable individual holds power in his hands', so we have a sibling society, a mass society with problems of obedience leading to feelings either of omnipotence or powerlessness in the crowd. In particular, such a society has problems in dealing with our constitutional bisexuality in that the homosexual

[1] A. Mitscherlich, *Society without the Father* (Tavistock Publications, London, 1969).

component is no longer bounded by authority father-figures that relate to the early father/son situation. Mitscherlich thus gives another illustration of the way in which social structures not only have a social role to play, but they also have to provide adequate channels for the expression of deep instinctual impulses.

Mitscherlich's book also brings us into the area of group interaction where our knowledge is much less far advanced than in the case of our understanding of the two-person interactions of individual psychotherapy. Some situations have well-established social roles for people to use, if only as spectators. The criminal legal trial is an obvious case. The sensational reporting in the cheaper Sunday papers is often regarded as reprehensible, but such stories usually have the proper moral ending of the criminal receiving deserved justice. The reader may alternately identify with the 'goodies' and the 'baddies', and it is an open question whether the vicarious enactment of forbidden sexual and aggressive fantasies by reading about them may not actually do more good than harm. However, the guilt-laden inquisitorial atmosphere of a legal trial reinforces only one way of dealing with unacceptable and largely unconscious impulses; namely, repressing them in one way or another. There are more constructive ways of dealing with our more primitive feelings.

Literature and drama are the obvious ways in which many people deepen the psychological understanding of themselves. The continuing vitality of old plays from Euripides to Shakespeare is proof of their value. The trouble is, of course, that very often we can be so little emotionally identified with the characters in second-rate novels or transitory plays that their activities are seen as pure entertainment, not as involving ourselves. Entertainment is a harmless enough activity in itself, and I am not criticizing people who go to the theatre just for that purpose. The contemporary theatre, however, requires much more audience participation. At times it shades into psycho-drama. This is a term coined by Moreno,[1] who was one of the pioneers of this method of treating psychological disorders. It had a considerable vogue in the 1950s, but for one reason or another has largely dropped out in the purely psychiatric setting, though still important 'on the fringe'. There are many possible variations, but, in essence, a group of patients in discussion formulate a theme that bears on the particular psychological problems of one or more members of that group—perhaps, for example, it is some variation on the eternal triangle, or a conflict between the generations. Some members of the group choose to improvise a scene in front of the rest of the group who can comment on the various interpretations of the roles that can be made. Because so many apparently diverse human situations contain elements in common, the classic dramas, going back as far as the Greeks, still have a tremendous hold on contemporary audiences. They can, however, slowly rigidify into some sort of ritual and lose their psychological impact. To an extent the case-history has

[1] J. L. Moreno began his work in Vienna where he was much influenced in the 1920s by the experimental theatre movement. His attempts to translate this movement into actual treatment took place later in the United States. For a short historical account see Walter Bromberg, *The Mind of Man: A History of Psychotherapy and Psychoanalysis* (first published by Harper, New York, 1937; later reissued as a Harper Torchbook).

replaced the parable as the teaching paradigm, as we see in these very lectures, but the formal teaching situation, with lectern and proper distance between the audience and myself, imposes constraints on our communication. Were I more imaginative, it might have been possible to put over what I have to say about public ritual more effectively with audience participation and videotape, but to have done so in even as many as three lectures would inevitably have given only the transient and superficial emotional atmosphere of a series of revivalist evangelical meetings.

We may seem at this point to have wandered far away from the concept of the counsellor as a man or woman working directly with one client at a time, or, at any rate, with members of a family in direct personal contact, with no more theatrical props than the tables and chairs—perhaps a couch—of the office. Counsellors and actors are but two examples of the men and women who deal with the largely unconscious forces that underly social activity. Sorcerers, soothsayers, oracles, and psycho-analysts usually occupy a rather fringe position in society and are often suspected of personal peculiarities and deviationist tendencies from the currently accepted mores. Up to a point, this is true, and many of them become more and more isolated and idiosyncratic. The psychic dangers of the job are obvious, since they have not just to listen to, but be emotionally involved in, and yet keep their distance from, primitive fantasies of love and hate that are at times intolerably violent. It is understandable that there is a large lunatic fringe around the responsible and well-trained members of the various professional organizations concerned with treatment. A counsellor on his own can easily lose heart, or at any rate lose his head in the welter of stresses to which he is exposed. Christ sent his disciples out two by two, and most psychoanalysts are very reluctant to settle in towns and cities on their own! The Church has always found mystics and spiritual directors awkward to fit into the bureaucracy; they prefer the relative obscurity of a monastic cell to the bishop's stall.

So far, I have apparently said little or nothing about religion in the conventional sense, and the part that it plays in society and in the life of individuals. Many people would, of course, say that religion is involved in every aspect of man's life, both individually and collectively; but it seems to me helpful to turn to social anthropology and to use Nadel's[1] division of the roles of religion into 'four major competences' (by this he means that religion *can* do the following things, though they can all be done by alternatives). Firstly, religion contributes to cosmology—man's view of the whole universe; secondly, it contributes to moral values; thirdly, it holds together social structures, whether this refers to a whole society as in the extreme case of a theocratic state, or to the millenarial role of sects of social outcasts. Lastly, it provides certain specific psychological experiences, usually of a so-called mystical character, though it must be noted that in practice few people who call themselves otherwise religious actually experience 'the thrill', in William James's phrase, or 'ecstasy', as discussed by Marghanita Laski.[2]

[1] S. F. Nadel, *Nupe Religion* (Routledge & Kegan Paul, London, 1954).
[2] Marghanita Laski, *Ecstasy* (Barrie & Jenkins, 1961).

For what is popularly supposed to be a dying art, religion has always occupied a remarkable proportion of the time and interest of sociologists, anthropologists, and psychologists. From these studies we have a much clearer idea of the social influences on the rise and fall of particular religious ways of life. For example, thanks to the work of many authors, but most recently Norman Cohn,[1] we know a good deal about the social structure of the extremist evangelical millenarial sects and their connection with the rootless lower middle class. More recently, Mary Douglas[2] has developed some ideas about the situations in which a secular world view develops. She contrasts the 'group', which refers to a body of people having certain common functions, be it at work or place of living; and the ego-centred 'grid' which refers to a status and role as described, for example, by kinship. She regards a secular world view not just as an inevitable modern development outgrowing primitive religion, but as occurring whenever group boundaries are weak and the ego-focused grid is strong. I quote, 'For the man who is uncommitted to any social group can make less use of the essentially bounded character of the human body to express his social concerns . . . he does not separate mind from matter, still less revere one or despise the other. He is strictly secular in outlook.'

Likewise, what seems to be a more advanced, enlightened doctrine of sin appears merely as the usual expression of a less differentiated experience of social

[1] Norman Cohn, *The Pursuit of the Millenium* (republished by Paladin Books, London, 1970).

[2] Mary Douglas, *Natural Symbols* (Barrie & Rockliffe: The Crescent Press, London, 1970).

relations: 'The more that social relations are differentiated by grid and group, the more the private individual is exhorted to pour his passions into prescribed channels, or control them altogether.'

Mary Douglas also attempts to apply Basil Bernstein's[1] ideas on elaborated and restricted speech codes to religious behaviour, especially ritual. The elaborated code requires complex planning and is more universal and abstract. The restricted code is much more part of the immediate social structure; utterances may convey information, but they also express a social structure and are oddly reminiscent of Hughlings Jackson's antithesis to propositional speech; namely, emotional speech. The line between prose and poetry, though hard to define, is drawn somewhere in the same region. There is a sense in which ritual is mainly a non-verbal, restricted code of communication. In one sense, such a restricted code may seem more primitive, but it is also more human in that it relates directly back to the earliest forms of human communication between the human baby and its family long before words can imperfectly express what is going on.

In trying to discern, therefore, what may be missing now that the traditional churches are emptying, we must put away the idea that the apparent decline of organized religion is an inevitable part of progress in the eighteenth- and nineteenth-century senses. Society, without a major role ascribed to organized religion, is a different society. It is not necessarily better or worse

[1] Basil Bernstein, 'A Socio-linguistic Approach to Social Learning', in J. Gould (ed.), *Penguin Survey of the Social Sciences* (Penguin Books, Harmondsworth, 1965).

morally, nor is it more true or false as regards human nature, but one making a different kind of person from one with a religious basis. Our advancing knowledge in so many scientific fields does mean that certain aspects of religious thought and behaviour can never come back unchanged. For example, our scientific understanding and increasing control of nature, other than man himself, means that this can no longer be an area on to which human problems can be projected. There is no place now for blessing the crops or cursing the weather. The doctrines of religion, especially as regards cosmology, must have some sort of psychological credibility.

Quite a number of profoundly original scientists have been either conventionally religious, or in some cases belonged to extreme sects. We may consider, for example, Michael Faraday's adherence to Sandemanianism, and Isaac Newton's later theological speculations. This splitting of the public scientific and the private religious aspects of the personality becomes, of course, increasingly untenable as the scientific interests of the individual verge more on the psychological and sociological sciences than the biological and physical.

The purposes for which people may still want to come together in the temple can be considered using Nadel's fourfold division. Beginning with his last point—will it be just for something that is akin to a personal religious experience which is currently sought by many people, young and old, sometimes using the short cut of drugs, and at times reminiscent of the antics of the dervishes? The anti-intellectualist dangers of isolating this aspect of religion are obvious, and the Church has traditionally been highly suspicious of all visions, emanations, and extreme states of ecstasy, as ends in themselves.

Will it be just for the sharing at the deepest level of personal griefs and triumphs? Death, treated as only a private grief without any public acceptance of mourning, can be an intolerable burden. The social importance of marriage is such that even strictly atheist states, like Russia, have had to go to slightly comical lengths to impress on young couples the solemnity and seriousness of the vows that they are taking. The human crises of birth, adulthood, marriage, parenthood, and bereavement, cannot be coped with rationally and formally with an elaborated code, since these events are inevitably tied to the deepest core of our experiences—we are back again to the suffering body.

Efforts to produce a humanist church from Robespierre to Solzhenitsyn are usually laughable in their crudity (as of course Solzhenitsyn recognizes). The solemnity and stained glass tend to stay, but because these attempts, by and large, adopt a moralistic and optimistic post-Rousseau view of man's nature as being essentially perfectible by social means, they have nothing to offer those aware of their internal contradictions—and creativeness.

At the other end of the socio-psychological continuum is Nadel's third point—the relation of religion to the corporate state. At present one sees little demand for a religious sanction of the State, or indeed of any sense of social solidarity with groups smaller than the nation. Yet there is an important sense in which the larger the social group, the more it needs the check of a religious organization that is an independent critic of it, rather than the support that an established church usually provides. The General Confession has become an even more empty ritual than private confession, but with it has gone an important sense in which groups should have a social mechanism for the acknowledgement of group responsibility.

It is in considering Nadel's first point—the relation of religion to cosmology—that I think we get to the heart of the matter. The word, 'cosmology', is perhaps unfortunate in that today it refers mainly to the vast physical universe of stars and nebulae. What Nadel really refers to is—What makes sense of the universe? And the answer to this question is more related to what we think about ourselves than about the stars. Scientists these days are rather more modest than they used to be; their theories of the universe are seen as model-building, a more limited aim than explaining away the universe. More than one model may be needed to help understand a single phenomenon. Concepts of physiology and psychology may seem quite different, but both are appropriate in helping us to understand a piece of human behaviour. At the extreme, each man should build his own model of the universe as his view of it is unique and cannot be reducible to others' viewpoints; but the scientific usefulness of a theory depends on its communicability. Whenever we deal with the nature of man and his relationship to society, the position is less clear. Psychologists, sociologists, anthropologists, philosophers, and theologians all make their contributions. Learned multi-disciplinary conference proceedings regularly get published, but there is still much confusion which obviously I am not going to solve within the next few paragraphs.

The counsellor's view of all this may seem rather irrelevant, but I believe there is a small contribution to be made from looking at what goes on in psychological treatment. In a group-treatment situation there are acted out, from time to time, some of the fundamental experiences—birth, death, bereavement, suffering. If these are not capable of being symbolized in our society, then they will be put away as increasingly unimportant and with them, I believe, goes man's essential humanity. Every society, except an intolerable, static, self-satisfied Utopia, will have tensions in it, potentially destructive and/or potentially creative. They cannot, without danger, be projected on to illness, crime, or social welfare, or whatever. Psychologists, apart from Jungians, have been rather suspicious of the idea of the collective unconscious. It certainly is a woolly idea, but in a recent dialogue[1] between anthropologists and psychologists the need for some concept like it to straddle the personal unconscious and hidden social forces was acknowledged. We need to accept and understand social forces at this deep level if we are to prevent a total fragmentation of our society, with the result that the artist would communicate only with his cult group, and the religious guru be shut up in his cell. Under these circumstances, power will certainly fall into the hands of the machines and the mass organizations that are necessary to provide us with the material

[1] Philip Mayer (ed.), *Socialization: The Approach from Social Anthropology* (A.S.A. Monog. No. 8, Tavistock Publications, London, 1970), chapter by G. Jahoda.

benefits of our civilization but which should not become our masters.

We need to express these unconscious forces by condensed symbols of ritual, but, at the same time, make sure that these symbols are open-ended and capable of creative new development. To put it in current religious terms, after the demythologization that culminated in the Death-of-God school, we need to remythologize our deepest human fantasies. The need for the symbolic representation of these human experiences can, I think, be best put over by an artistic analogy. In that divine charade, *The Magic Flute*, which contains some of the profoundest of all music, we have an allegory. Poor Papageno is terrified in the last act; he is going through the purifications with Tamino, not really knowing what is happening, but joining in their beneficent effect. The emotional intensity needed to influence people in this way appears to occur only in intimate groups meeting successively over periods of time. Today, we are so suspicious of the possible bad ends to which such groups can be directed, that we are in danger of leaving men and women, especially at the impressionable younger ages, without experience needed for the growth of adult maturity.

The rituals of rebirth by trial occur constantly in many religions; as Ehrenzweig[1] points out, the dying-god theme explicitly refers to the inner psychological meaning of incarnation and resurrection. Mozart's opera illustrates the point that artistic genius need not

[1] Anton Ehrenzweig, *The Hidden Order of Art* (Paladin Books, London, 1970).

imply philosophical depth. No comprehensive cosmology can be deduced from the pseudo-archaeological piffle that forms the exiguous theoretical background of Freemasonry. The insights into human salvation of Mozart's librettist, Schikaneder, are innocent of any idea of cosmic creation and redemption. It takes the combined efforts of Schiller and Beethoven in the Ninth Symphony to raise these questions at the same artistic intensity as Mozart gives to the purely human drama. The failure of religion today to provide a dynamic creative view of human nature that does justice to its dark side is more important than its failure to give 'moral leadership'. In the Christian view, only the resurrection experience of 'being born again', is the answer to existential pessimism. Any afternoon in Out-patients will provide the empirical evidence that led our more gloomy ancestors to elaborate doctrines of original sin and predestination. But unless we can reconstruct our own psychological past in terms that are shared by others in art and religion, then our private world becomes sterile. However satisfying and interesting this may be to ourselves, it is of no value even to our immediate family.

There is thus, in my view, some special tie-up between counselling and religion that is strangely undervalued in recent sociological studies of religion.[1] Both

[1] For example, Bryan Wilson's *Religion in a Secular Society* (Pelican series, Penguin Books, Harmondsworth, 1966) has no reference to anything psychological, while Betty R. Scharf in *The Sociological Study of Religion* (Hutchinson University Library, London, 1970) has a short passage on out-of-date views of Freud. Roland Robertson's *The Sociological Interpretation of Religion* (Blackwell's Sociology Series, Oxford, 1970) does have about three pages on 'religion in relation to psychiatry and psychology', but gives the impression that this relationship is

are concerned in a special way with man helping to understand himself and his relationship to the universe. Up to now, counsellors have, I think, been able to avoid the issue of their group responsibility. Behind many a psychotherapist there lurks an anarchist identifying with his client's problems and seeing the world from the client's point of view only. Yet a proper group role might in some ways look like the early church. At first, counsellor and client have to withdraw from society to get the necessary distance from every-day life that allows the deeper levels of personal inter-action needed for healing. As soon as such methods get institutionalized and accepted, we have power and authority in the world—but Heaven forbid the day when the Department of Social Welfare has an office as grand as a cathedral! In due course, counsellors may find themselves shaking hands with Dostoievsky's Grand Inquisitor. Yet somehow knowledge has to be handed on, and this requires scholarship, teaching, and management, which we cannot avoid, though the prophets amongst us will always be uncomfortably on the fringe. What I am trying to make clear is a distinc-tion between any professional structure for counselling comparable to other professional bodies for medicine and law, and the role of a church which embraces all members of society but which, I believe, has a special relation with counselling. The Church's function is more than just intellectual criticism of the moral values

peripheral and unimportant. In part these attitudes are a reflection of the chronic and widespread failure of communication between academic psychologists and sociologists already referred to. The approach of social anthropologists like Mary Douglas is in general broader and more comprehensive.

of society. It has a sacramental role, acting out the inevitable creative and destructive tensions and myths that groups generate.[1] I hope my remark at the beginning of the first lecture about the three strands in the use of the term Corpus Christi now makes sense—the body of flesh and blood, the social body, and the sacramental body. I want now to say some more about the origins of these myths that join the strands together.

The raw materials out of which new myths are created consist of bodily functions and feelings on one side, and the here-and-now environment on the other. The latter has two parts—human society as already created by man, and the world of nature. The latter, up until very recently, at any rate, had entirely shaped our lives by the rhythm of the seasons and the fear of natural catastrophes like famines and epidemics. The still relatively unchanged parts of the raw material are our own bodily functions—birth, death, the curve of tension, satisfaction, and relaxation—that is a deeply ingrained biological pattern seen in oral, excretory, and sexual behaviour. As long as man is recognizably a human being as we know him, these facts of life will always remain our first and deepest experiences, influencing profoundly how we see the world.

A baby's first sense of an Other outside itself begins as a complex of tactile, olfactory, and other bodily sensations. It needs to create, or rather re-create, the certainty that the curve of tension, gratification, relaxation from feeding and bodily functions will be

[1] R. A. Lambourne's *Community, Church and Healing* (Darton, Longman & Todd, London, 1963) contains a well-worked-out description of the Church's healing roles in contemporary England, written some years before community mental health was a popular concept.

maintained. The solution to this problem colours the adult's subsequent view of life. Hutten[1] shows convincingly how this life view can be seen even in the predilections of scientists for one type of theory rather than another; for example, the difficulties that many have in accepting probabilistic rather than deterministic theories. The hard objective fact so beloved of scientists has the psychological qualities of the permanence of the breast. The scientist creates order in the world outside in the same way that the artist creates a painting—cosmology is essentially a model-building process.

Modern existentialist philosophers, and theologians influenced by them, adopt much the same line to the religious Other.[2] Sin is etymologically derived from the same word as sunder. Perhaps it is now better translated by alienation. Similarly, the World, in the derogatory sense, corresponds to the depersonalized, dehumanized collectivity of Heidegger, that well deserves the scorn poured on it by Marcuse, amongst others. The religious—or, at any rate, the Christian—affirmation is essentially a positive and optimistic existentialism. Tillich speaks of grace as of being grasped by it. There are echoes of the baby at the breast enfolded in mother's arms. If, early on in our lives, we can be sure that the

[1] Ernest M. Hutten, *The Origins of Science* (George Allen & Unwin, London, 1962).

[2] John Macquarrie, *Studies in Christian Existentialism* (S.C.M. Press, London, 1965) contains useful analyses of contemporary theological thinking. I am indebted to David L. Edwards (in *Religion and Change*, Hodder & Stoughton, London, 1969) for Bultmann's aphorism, 'The question of God and the question of myself are identical.' This is very like the approach of the sociologist, Peter Berger, in the chapter, 'Starting with Man' in *A Rumour of Angels* (Allen Lane, the Penguin Press, London, 1969). The Durkheimian view that God and Society are one is being replaced by a more individualistic view, even in sociological circles.

Other is real, solid, and ever present, then we shall later be more sure that there is another Being. This is precisely the psychological point at which the Incarnation is such a revolutionary psychological experience. To be able to tie the essence of the world to such a paradigmatic experience cannot fail to have a profound liberating influence. Unfortunately, for centuries, 'Jesus saves' has been interpreted often too literally, and an intense psychological experience regarded as the *sine qua non* of conversion. For a short while before the war, at any rate around Hampstead, 'Are you saved?', was replaced by, 'Have you been analysed?', as the evangelical challenge, with much the same hollow answer. 'I am the Way', the pilgrimage idea, is nearer the truth. In the most existentialist sense we cannot prove that the Way is true or not, and all sorts of personality differences may enter into the acceptance or rejection of such an idea, with some favouring the more atheistic and pessimistic existentialism of, for example, Jean Paul Sartre. At least, one can say that the most creative artists have in some way been religious in the sense of being aware of a living Other.

Nature, as something with which man must come to terms, is less obtrusive in our scientific age, unless we wilfully destroy it ourselves by biological or nuclear means. Thus, parables based on agricultural metaphors, such as the Sower and the Seed, no longer have such immediate and satisfying relevance—the more's the pity, perhaps. There is no need for propitiation, for blessing and cursing, except for that which is inside ourselves. There is no longer something outside ourselves which is largely hostile and out of control. There is no screen on which to project man's inner problems, nor any arena in which to enact them other than that which we can ourselves create. In a way, the Bible foresaw this as it begins in the Garden of Eden and ends in the City of New Jerusalem.

There is a sense in which this process can be seen as a proper evolutionary step. The gradual emergence of higher forms of biological existence, as opposed to the physical world without life, has led to organisms creating, in Claude Bernard's famous phrase, 'the constancy of the internal milieu'. Man can now wilfully do this for his external milieu as well. The myth of Prometheus reminds us, of course, that in saying this, I have said nothing new nor discovered the psychic dangers. These dangers have, however, to be constantly reiterated, even in a society which has suddenly become rather disenchanted with the dubious blessings of science. Our terrifying freedom to play the Creator has always been seen as a somewhat mixed blessing, but it is inevitable.

I should like to turn now to discuss briefly some of the implications of our new powers for the older and newer professions. In general, all of us who belong to the traditional, somewhat authoritarian professions, find ourselves no longer able to tell our patients how to lead their lives. We are sharing in the general flattening of the pyramid of authority that is cheered or feared according to whether you are under or over twenty-five years of age. As the Church's pamphlet on problems of dying well puts it, 'Increasingly, decisions are made by the doctor *with* and not *for* their patients.' Most psychotherapists have been aware of this and insist that they never give advice, but only try to help their clients to see why they want to remain in a dependent situation.

Self-determination also lies behind many changes in the law as regards suicide, abortion, and probably, in due course, euthanasia. One of the effects of these changes in medicine and law is that man can less easily project his internal difficulties on to the areas of disturbance traditionally controlled by these professions. Neurotic dependence on a doctor, dressed up as an 'illness', requiring medical treatment, is no longer possible once both the patient and the doctor realize the nature of their psychological interaction. The role of legal sanctions should be to force the individual back to his own resources of personal control.

More of the burden of carrying the inadequate and the dependent will thus be thrown on to the counselling and welfare professions, whether they like it or not. Perhaps some of the anxiety and restiveness detected in recent recruits to the social services reflect their partial awareness of their inadequate personality resources to carry emotional burdens that doctors have always had when assuming responsibility for the life and death of their patients, and not just the cure of their illnesses. The strain on them is all the greater because they cannot share the authority and prestige of an ancient profession.

It is now time to come back to our patient, William. Traditional medicine and law respectively see his disturbance only incompletely in terms of madness or badness. Similarly, there are the obvious limitations to the concept of maladjustment in contemporary social work and psychology. There is also a sense in which William was right in thinking that it is society that is sick and not he. But it is difficult to weave together the various strands that make up the creative aspect of William's crisis. To a greater extent than most patients, he is looking for wholeness—a new integration of his personality—so that in this sense he has an intrapsychic problem. We know very well that few, if any, persons can fully achieve this, and the unintegrated parts of his personality may appear as symptoms in a narrow medical sense, or as bits of perverse, even delinquent, behaviour. To separate the bad parts off completely as 'medical' or 'delinquent' is, however, to deny the ideal of the wholeness. Society needs a myth and a corresponding social structure for understanding and forgiving those who are not whole, rather than be content to see them as ill, maladjusted, or delinquent. This is the sacramental concept embodied in Corpus Christi, and is something often expressed in religious words. The psychological experience of healing accompanying it is dramatically described as, 'Except that ye are born again, ye cannot enter the Kingdom of Heaven.'

Ehrenzweig discusses rebirth in relationship to *The Magic Flute*, to which I have already alluded. The self-creating principle is shown in a minor part—that of the boys who zigzag through that mad charade, just as in a dream a minor incident may be the most important key to the latent content. The boys epitomize creativity in the sense of something new that seems to have no antecedents and which can have immense destructive possibilities of the old order, social and/or personal. The Promethean myth refers explicitly to this.

Thus, my conclusion is that counselling must be, in a certain sense, related to the way in which society views itself as a whole. Though ill defined, this view has to be to some extent religious in that the symbols of rebirth and redemption are fundamental. It is not a question of psychiatry replacing religion, nor of religion replacing psychiatry. In an open society dedicated to self-fulfilment of all its members, no narrow or partial view of the aims of counselling can be satisfactory.

What sort of religion and how it is expressed in our mobile society of mass communication, is another matter. The historical position of Christianity is not something on which I can comment in the context of these lectures. I am more concerned to show how some of the hard, obscure, and oracular utterances of the Bible and other ancient scriptures still have psychological validity, however demythologized. It is, I think, no accident that the most advanced theory and practice of counselling have arisen in the countries which have the most liberal and anti-hierarchical form of Western Christianity. I have already mentioned Halmos's stress on the Christian overtone of the whole profession, whether practised by people who call themselves Christians or not. These lectures are offered as a small contribution to what I hope will be an ongoing public debate on the role of counselling in our society.